Advanced Coloring Book

LEGENDS

MW01538206

About

Would you like to feel the brush strokes of legendary painters? Guessing what they think at that moment? Put yourself in their shoes and have fun.

Using color science, we know the way to express a **photorealistic** picture in just **5 colors**. We reduced the number of colors of the **20** paintings from **legendary painters** using this special method and made it possible for you to paint by assigning letters to each color. Get ready to put in **309.429 colored dots** :)

How to?

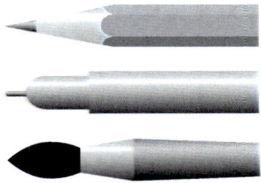

Choose the painting tool that suits you best

R G B Y K

Finding a pen/pencil set or ink containing all 5 colors will make your job easier

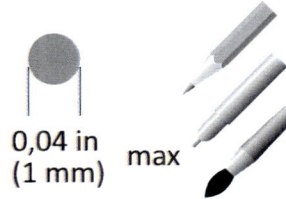

0,04 in (1 mm) max

The tip size should be max. 0,04 in (1 mm)

Each letter symbolizes a color

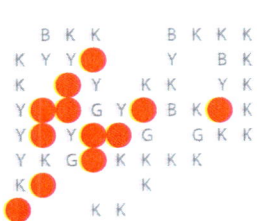

R

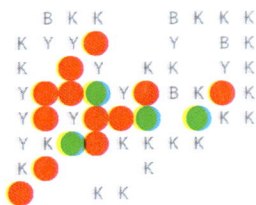

G

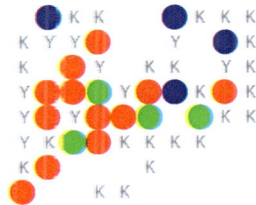

B

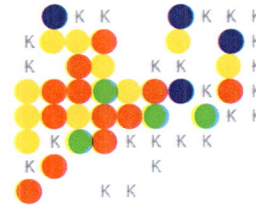

Y

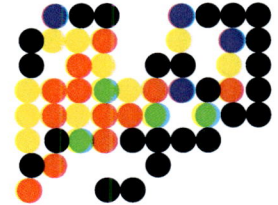

K

11.040 Dots

Alfred Sisley
French, 1839 - 1899
Flood at Port-Marly, 1872
Oil on canvas

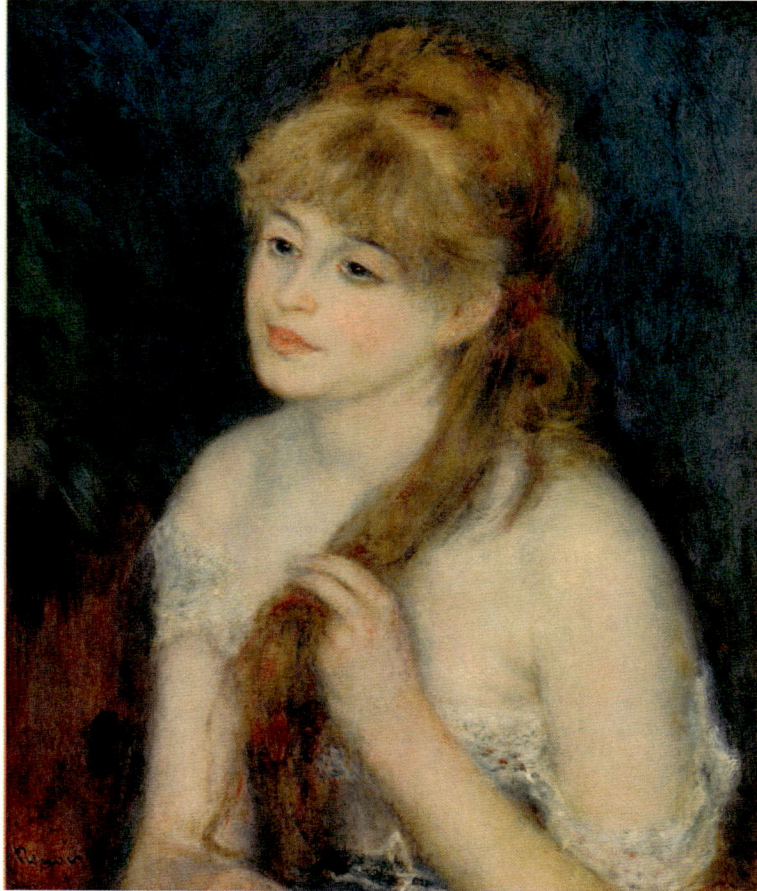

17.908 Dots

Auguste Renoir
French, 1841 - 1919
Young Woman Braiding Her Hair, 1876
Oil on canvas

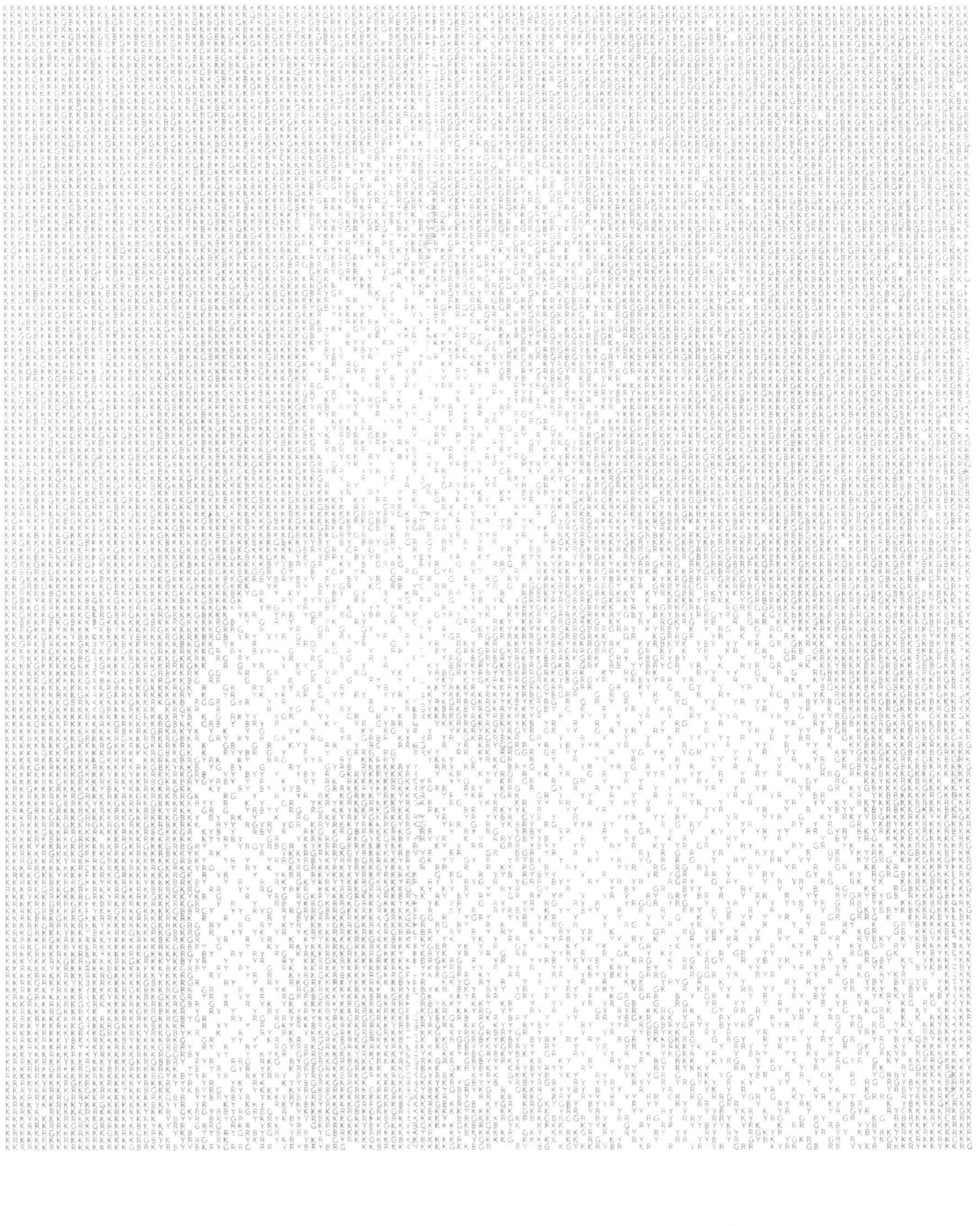

14.893 Dots

Berthe Morisot
French, 1841 - 1895
The Artist's Sister at a Window, 1869
Oil on canvas

12.494 Dots

Camille Pissarro
French, 1830 - 1903
Bridge at Caracas, 1854
Watercolor over graphite

16.682 Dots

Claude Monet
French, 1840 - 1926
Bazille and Camille (Study for "Déjeuner sur l'Herbe"), 1865
Oil on canvas

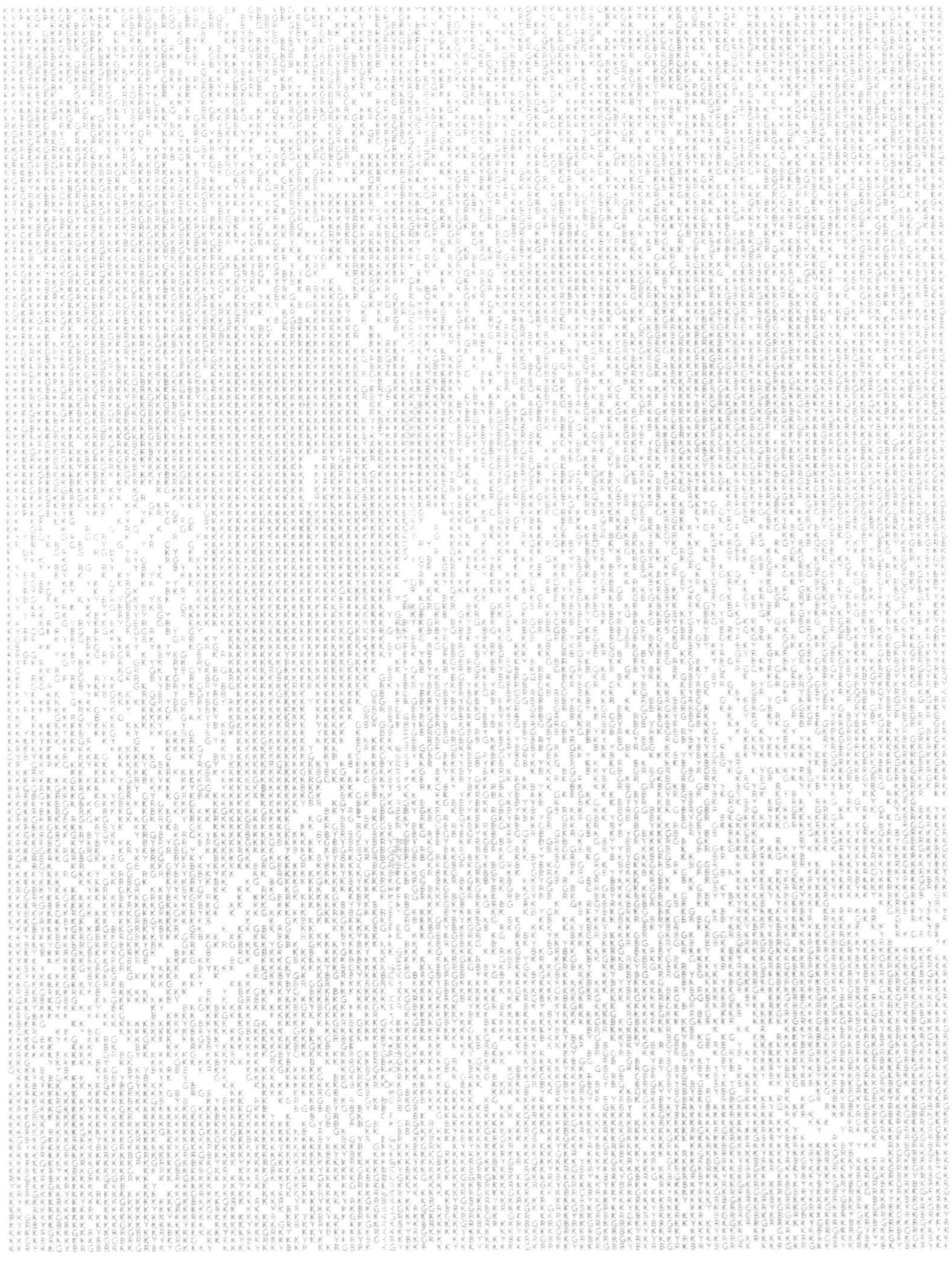

20.832 Dots

Edgar Degas
French, 1834 - 1917
René de Gas, 1855
Oil on canvas

13.624 Dots

Edouard Manet
French, 1832 - 1883
The Railway, 1873
Oil on canvas

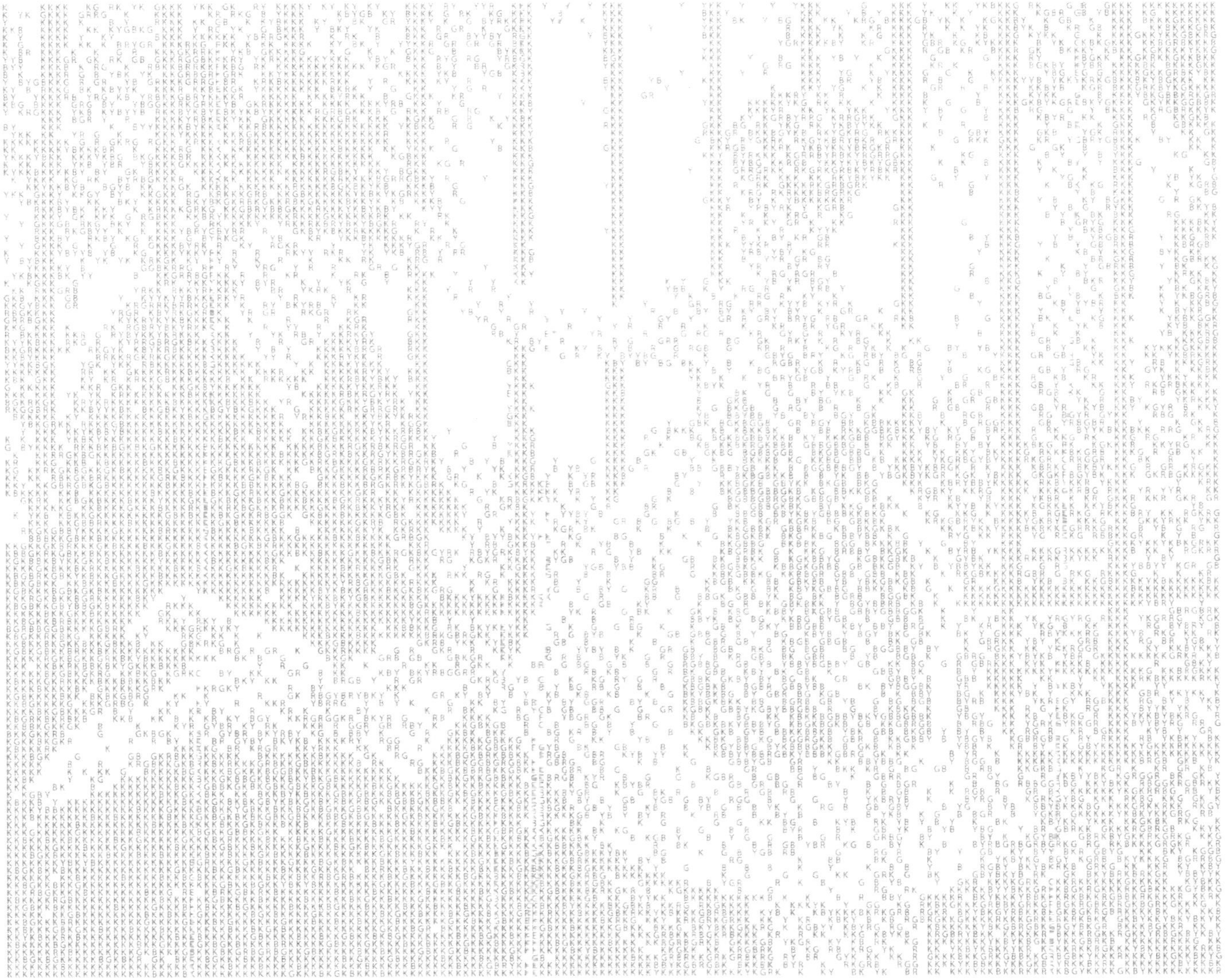

8.275 Dots

Eugène Boudin
French, 1824 - 1898
Two Ladies Seated and a Couple Walking on the Beach, c. 1866
Watercolor over graphite on wove paper

17.449 Dots

Eugène Delacroix
French, 1798 - 1863
Tiger and Snake, 1862
Oil on canvas

18.105 Dots

Eva Gonzalès
French, 1849 - 1883
Nanny and Child, 1877/1878
Oil on canvas

18.177 Dots

Frans Hals
Dutch, c. 1582/1583 - 1666
Portrait of a Member of the Haarlem Civic Guard, c. 1636/1638
Oil on canvas

16.623 Dots

Frédéric Bazille
French, 1841 - 1870
Edmond Maître, 1869
Oil on canvas

11.934 Dots

Georges Seurat
French, 1859 - 1891
Peasant with a Hoe, c. 1882
Oil on wood

15.096 Dots

Gustave Caillebotte
French, 1848 - 1894
Skiffs, 1877
Oil on canvas

12.918 Dots

Henri Rousseau
French, 1844 - 1910
Boy on the Rocks, 1895/1897
Oil on linen

20.274 Dots

Leonardo da Vinci
Florentine, 1452 - 1519
Ginevra de' Benci [obverse], c. 1474/1478
Oil on panel

17.604 Dots

Paul Cézanne
French, 1839 - 1906
The Peppermint Bottle, 1893/1895
Oil on canvas

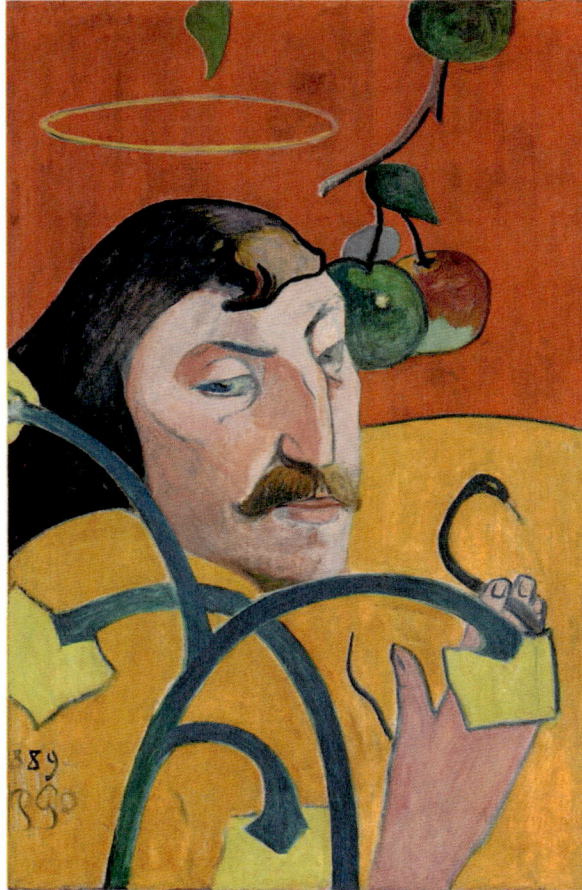

13.976 Dots

Paul Gauguin
French, 1848 - 1903
Self-Portrait, 1889
Oil on wood

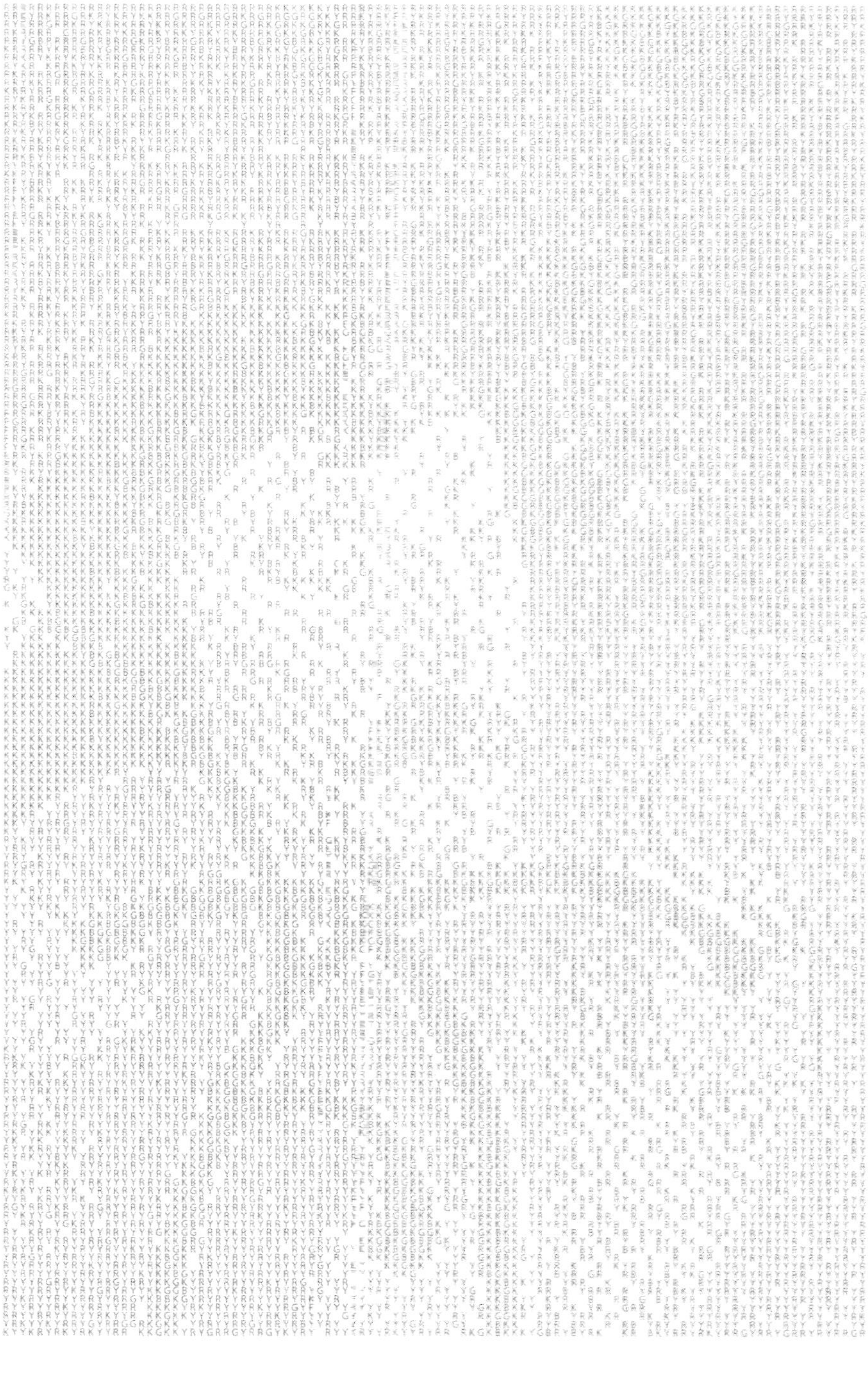

14.534 Dots

Raphael
Marchigian, 1483 - 1520
The Niccolini-Cowper Madonna, 1508
Oil on panel

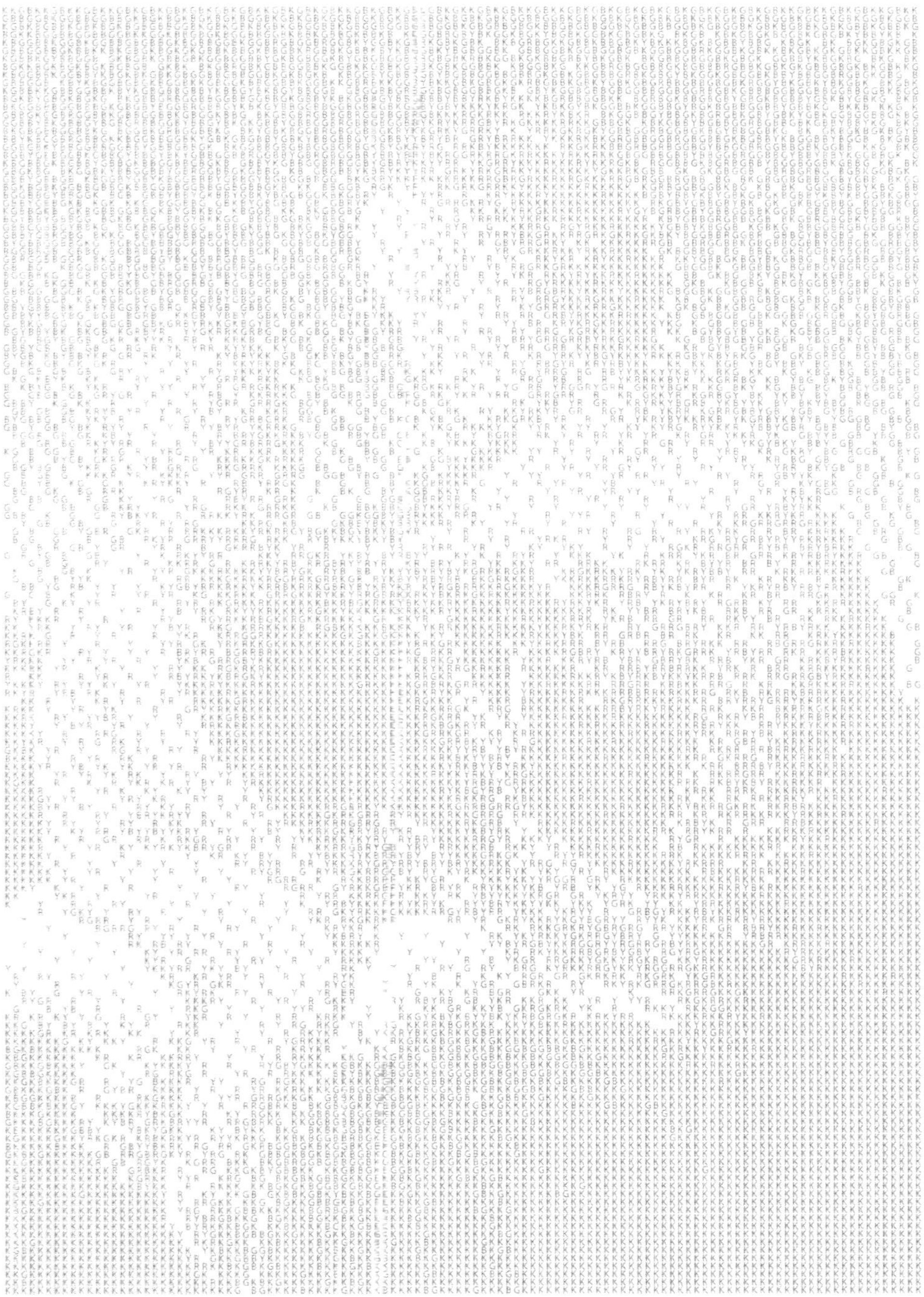

16.991 Dots

Vincent van Gogh
Dutch, 1853 - 1890
Self-Portrait, 1889
Oil on canvas

Made in the USA
Las Vegas, NV
14 September 2023